MY PLACE IN HISTORY

My Life During the GOLD RUSH

By Max Caswell

Gareth Stevens Publishing

Please visit our website, www.garethstevens.com. For a free color catalog of all our high-quality books, call toll free 1-800-542-2595 or fax 1-877-542-2596.

Library of Congress Cataloging-in-Publication Data

Names: Caswell, Max, author.
Title: My life during the Gold Rush / Max Caswell.
Description: New York : Gareth Stevens Publishing, [2018] | Series: My place in history | Includes index.
Identifiers: LCCN 2017008901| ISBN 9781538202975 (pbk. book) | ISBN 9781538202982 (6 pack) | ISBN 9781538202999 (library bound book)
Subjects: LCSH: California–Gold discoveries–Juvenile literature. | California–History–1846-1850–Juvenile literature. | Frontier and pioneer life–California–Juvenile literature.
Classification: LCC F865 .C325 2018 | DDC 979.4/03–dc23
LC record available at https://lccn.loc.gov/2017008901

Published in 2018 by
Gareth Stevens Publishing
111 East 14th Street, Suite 349
New York, NY 10003

Designer: Bethany Perl
Editor: Joan Stoltman

Photo credits: Cover, p. 1 (miner at riverbed) General Photographic Agency/Getty Images; cover, p. 1 (background) Natalia Sheinkin/Shutterstock.com; cover, pp. 1–24 (torn strip) barbaliss/Shutterstock.com; cover, pp. 1–24 (photo frame) Davor Ratkovic/Shutterstock.com; cover, pp. 1–24 (white paper) HABRDA/Shutterstock.com; cover, pp. 1–24 (parchment) M. Unal Ozmen/Shutterstock.com; cover, pp. 1–24 (textured edge) saki80/Shutterstock.com; pp. 1–24 (paper background) Kostenko Maxim/Shutterstock.com; p. 5 (old paper) Krasovski Dmitri/Shutterstock.com; p. 5 (gold nugget) Flugklick/Shutterstock.com; p. 5 (grunge texture) Lawkeeper/Shutterstock.com; p. 5 (river operations) Harper's Weekly magazine/Wikipedia.org; p. 7 (miners panning) Everett Historical/Shutterstock.com; p. 7 (panning close-up) Trueblackheart/Shutterstock.com; p. 9 (prospectors) MPI/Archive Photos/Getty Images; p. 9 (miner at a riverbed) Bettmann/Getty Images; p. 11 (ship deck) Rischgitz/Hulton Archive/Getty Images; p. 11 (miner ship) VCG Wilson/Corbis Historical/Getty Images; p. 13 SuperStock/Getty Images; p. 15 (gold rush photo) Spencer Weiner/Los Angeles Times/Getty Images; p. 15 (gambling) Interim Archives/Archive Photos/ Getty Images; p. 17 (San Francisco before) ullstein bild/Getty Images; p. 17 (San Francisco after) courtesy of the Library of Congress; p. 19 ZU_09/DigitalVision Vectors/Getty Images; p. 21 sibiranna/Shutterstock.com.

Printed in the United States of America

CPSIA compliance information: Batch #CS17GS: For further information contact Gareth Stevens, New York, New York at 1-800-542-2595.

CONTENTS

Words in the glossary appear in **bold** type the first time they are used in the text.

gold DISCOVERED!

April 2, 1848

Gold used to belong only to kings, but not anymore! Here in California, gold's free for the taking!

My mother's packed our home in San Francisco, and we're heading east. Only men are coming to mine, she says, leaving their wives and children behind. They'll need someone to do their laundry, she says. They don't know how! We'll set up shop right in a miners' camp. I'm leaving school for a while to go help, so this journal will help me practice handwriting.

Notes from History

Gold was discovered in California in a stream outside of Sacramento. Locals rushed in, and by 1854, one out of every 90 Americans would head to California to try their luck finding gold.

THE NEW YORK HERALD

NEW YORK, SATURDAY, AUGUST 19, 1848.

GOLD! GOLD! GOLD FROM THE AMERICAN RIVER!

Californians say 'Your streams have minnows, and ours are paved with gold.'

GOLD NUGGET

The *New York Herald* first printed the story of California gold in August 1848, and many other newspapers followed throughout that fall. But few people believed it until President James K. Polk announced that it was true in December.

Life Along THE RIVER

August 20, 1848

We've traveled 150 miles (240 km) east to a camp in the foothills of the Sierra Nevada run by two Irish brothers, the Murphys.

Boy, was my mother right! Before we arrived, the miners wore the same muddy clothes every day. They're grateful we've arrived—and willing to pay a pretty penny for our services! We make $120 a week. A woman named Lucy Stoddard Wakefield makes $240 a week selling pies! Other women offer meals and boarding, and all earn better wages than ever before.

Notes from History

The miners needed all sorts of businesses and services: laundries, places to eat, merchants, **transportation**, banking, housing, and **entertainment**. These businesses would make much more money than most of the miners ever would.

By 1850, 92 percent of the people in California were men.

These POOR MEN

November 8, 1848

At first, it seemed like everyone was finding gold—along the riverbanks, in the riverbed, and in every stream. Our first few months here, we heard of many striking it rich. The Murphy brothers gave us $400 to thank us after they found their fortune!

But the rest of these men are dirty, wet, cold, **exhausted**, and lonely. They dig from sunrise to sunset, crushing their fingernails digging all day by hand. These poor men have put their future in the hands of lady luck.

Notes from History

Before **prospecting**, miners needed to claim a piece of the land around the river. Their claim was made official by a claim officer, and then no one else could touch that land for a certain amount of time.

In the summer of 1848, fewer than 5,000 prospectors arrived, and they were mostly locals, including Native Americans and Mexicans.

They Came IN SHIPS

April 17, 1849

Ships are arriving from all over the world carrying gold seekers by the thousands. These people spend months at sea, so **desperate** to get here that they travel inside the dark, lower **cargo** decks of ships like cattle!

I heard about a ship where rats got into the food supply! A man last week told me that a strange, tropical illness killed many people aboard his ship when they went through South America. How frightening!

Notes from History

After ships arrived in San Francisco, crews often left boats right in the harbor and rushed off to find gold themselves. Parts of the city were built right on top of ships, including the *General Harrison*, a ship found underneath downtown San Francisco in 2001!

Over 40,000 people, mostly men, came by sea to California in 1849 alone! Many countries were experiencing war, unrest, or **famine** at the time, so the gold gave them hope for a better future.

BY LAND

August 29, 1849

I met an 11-year-old boy named James who came to California with his father from Chicago, Illinois, in search of gold. He said the trail was so bumpy it hurt to ride in the wagon, so everyone just walked—the whole way!

People keep arriving, but there's no more room! They're so tired when they arrive, and there's no shelter or rest here. Mother and I have a cabin, but there aren't even tents left for sale. Many people sleep under trees.

Notes from History

The way to California by land was more affordable than by sea, but not as quick. Land travel couldn't begin until after the spring, so many of the 42,000 people who came by land in 1849 arrived too late to find gold.

The gold rush brought people from 31 states and over 25 countries. It was one of the largest **migrations** in human history and the first time people from so many different **cultures** were all in one place.

Too Many People, TOO LITTLE GOLD

September 13, 1849

People arriving now are too late. There aren't any claims left, and whatever gold remains is deep in dirt and rocks. There's much stealing, lying, **gambling**, and cheating happening. There aren't laws or police to stop it.

A man in the next camp was murdered over a small piece of gold, so now I'm not allowed out of the cabin alone. My mother's scared we're going to get robbed, so we're taking a trip to San Francisco to bring our money to a bank.

Notes from History

That early gold from the riverbeds was there because thousands of years of weather had loosened the gold from the hard stone of the Sierra Nevada and washed it down the mountains.

GAMBLING

Claims were written so you only had a certain amount of time to work an area before another miner could claim that land. By the summer of 1849, very little land had been left unturned!

SAN FRANCISCO!

October 18, 1849

My hometown is unrecognizable! People have been spending gold as fast as they find it. I finally have a dinner that's not some form of hangtown fry, that meat-and-egg mix my mother makes every night back at camp.

We treated ourselves to a play, though we could have seen a bull fighting a grizzly bear, too. The play was about a love story, but I was too busy looking at the unbelievable costumes to follow it.

Notes from History

Miners mostly ate boiled potatoes, bacon, bread, beans, and eggs in camp. But if they found gold, food was one of the many things they would spend their gold on, especially French food.

San Francisco quickly became a major world port and the most **diverse** city in the world. In 1848, the city's population was 800. By 1853, it was over 50,000.

A New CAMP

April 12, 1850

Sorry I haven't written in awhile—I was enjoying San Francisco too much to write! So much has changed. The days where one man, or even 100 men, found gold with their own two hands are over.

Our new cabin is closer to the mountains because the only gold left now is for machines to find in the mountains, under forests, and deep beneath the earth. We've been hired by a company to provide laundry services for their 100 machine workers.

Notes from History

Once the surface gold was gone, a miner would need to **sift** through 160 buckets of dirt a day just to find an ounce of gold, or $10 to $16 worth of gold. This means they often couldn't afford food, let alone the trip back home!

Over $60 million worth of gold was found each year of the 1850s by companies that could afford the expensive machines used to crush stone.

The Rush IS OVER

June 1, 1850

I guess "gold fever" is cured. For Mother and her business friends, hard work meant money and success. But, sadly, most of these "49ers" didn't find what they came for. James and his father—and many others—can't afford to get home. They're headed to Sacramento or San Francisco. Maybe I'll see them when I get home!

Even though we're not millionaires like the Murphy brothers, my life will never be the same!

Notes from History

Failures were far more common than successes in the gold rush, but the tales of those successes would live on in history. California would forever be known as the "golden state."

Eureka! Successes During the Gold Rush

1848, Weber Creek
Two men find **$17,000** worth of gold in one week → That's about **$415,000** today!

1848
The Murphy brothers find **$1.5 MILLION** worth of gold → That's about **$37 MILLION** today!

1850, Rich Bar
Three German men dig up **$23 MILLION** worth of gold → That's about **$561 MILLION** today!

Over $2 billion, in the form of 750,000 pounds (340,194 kg) of gold, was found yearly during the California gold rush.

GLOSSARY

cargo: goods carried by a plane, train, truck, or ship

culture: the beliefs and ways of life of a group of people

desperate: very sad and upset because of having little or no hope

diverse: made up of unlike elements

entertainment: things that are interesting for people to watch or listen to

exhaust: to tire out or wear out someone completely

famine: a situation in which many people do not have enough food to eat

gambling: the act of playing a game in which money is at risk

migration: the act of moving from one country or place to live or work in another

prospect: to search an area for valued matter, such as gold

sift: to go through something very carefully in order to find something useful or valuable

transportation: a system for moving people or goods from one place to another

For more INFORMATION

Books

Hall, Brianna. *Strike It Rich! The Story of the California Gold Rush.* North Mankato, MN: Capstone Press, 2015.

Landau, Elaine. *The Gold Rush in California: Would You Catch Gold Fever?* Berkeley Heights, NJ: Enslow Elementary, 2015.

Shoup, Kate. *Life as a Prospector in the California Gold Rush.* New York, NY: Cavendish Square Publishing, 2017.

Websites

Major "Strikes" in the California Gold Rush
pbs.org/wgbh/amex/goldrush/map/index.html

Strike It Rich!
pbs.org/wgbh/amex/goldrush/sfeature/game.html
Choose a character and try to strike it rich in this online gold rush game!

Publisher's note to educators and parents: Our editors have carefully reviewed these websites to ensure that they are suitable for students. Many websites change frequently, however, and we cannot guarantee that a site's future contents will continue to meet our high standards of quality and educational value. Be advised that students should be closely supervised whenever they access the Internet.

INDEX